New Vanguard • 134

Red SAM:
The SA-2 Guideline
Anti-Aircraft Missile

Steven J Zaloga • Illustrated by Jim Laurier

First published in Great Britain in 2007 by Osprey Publishing,
Midland House, West Way, Botley, Oxford OX2 0PH, UK
443 Park Avenue South, New York, NY 10016, USA
E-mail: info@ospreypublishing.com

A CIP catalog record for this book is available from the British Library

ISBN: 978 1 84603 062 8

Page layout by: Melissa Orrom Swan, Oxford
Index by Margaret Vaudrey
Typeset in Helvetica Neue and ITC New Baskerville
Originated by PPS Grasmere Ltd, Leeds, UK
Printed in China through Worldprint Ltd.

07 08 09 10 11   10 9 8 7 6 5 4 3 2 1

For a catalog of all books published by Osprey Military and Aviation
please contact:

NORTH AMERICA
Osprey Direct, c/o Random House Distribution Center, 400 Hahn Road,
Westminster, MD 21157
E-mail: info@ospreydirect.com

ALL OTHER REGIONS
Osprey Direct UK, P.O. Box 140 Wellingborough, Northants, NN8 2FA, UK
E-mail: info@ospreydirect.co.uk

www.ospreypublishing.com

Artist's note

Readers may care to note that the original paintings from which the color
plates in this book were prepared are available for private sale. All reproduction
copyright whatsoever is retained by the Publishers. All inquiries should be
addressed to:

Jim Laurier, P.O. Box 1118, Keene, New Hampshire, NH 03431, USA

The Publishers regret that they can enter into no correspondence upon
this matter.

Dedication

In Memory of LtCol Jim Loop, whose infectious enthusiasm got me interested
in missile history.

Author's note

The author would like to thank members of the staffs of Fakel and Almaz for
their help. Thanks also go to Wojciech Luczak, Ron Feldman, Lon Nordeen,
David Markhov, and Christopher Foss for help with photos and information
used in this book. Unattributed photos in this book are from the author's
collection and were provided by organizations and colleagues in Russia
and the former Soviet Union.

The Western and Russian designations SA-2 and S-75 are used
interchangeably in this book.

RED SAM: THE SA-2 GUIDELINE ANTI-AIRCRAFT MISSILE

SAM ORIGINS

The S-75 was the most important tactical missile system of the Cold War and played a central role in the evolution of modern air warfare. Better known by its Western intelligence designator as the SA-2 Guideline, it was originally developed for the strategic defense of major Soviet cities against US and British bomber attacks. It was first used in combat in the late 1950s and early 1960s against US U-2 spyplanes over Russia, China, and Cuba. As strategic weaponry evolved from long-range bombers to intercontinental missiles, the importance of the S-75 in strategic air defense diminished. The Soviet Union began exporting the S-75 to many of its client states, including Vietnam, Egypt, and Syria. As a result, it played a pivotal role in the air wars over Vietnam in 1966–73, and in the Middle East in 1967, 1970, and 1973. The use of the S-75 in these air battles was the primary catalyst for the "wizard war" that resulted in many new innovations in electronic warfare, including the development of stealth technology. Although increasingly obsolete, the widespread export of the S-75 ensured that it was used in many other conflicts during the 1980s and 1990s.

The combination of long-range strategic bombers and the atomic bomb initiated the greatest revolution in warfare of the twentieth century. Instead of massive thousand-plane bombing raids, it became possible to destroy an entire city with a single bomber carrying a single nuclear bomb. Traditional defenses based on artillery and fighters became obsolete overnight since they could seldom defeat more than five to ten percent of the attacking bombers. In the nuclear age, this was completely unacceptable

The S-75 Dvina system was the world's first surface-to-air missile used in combat, revolutionizing air defense tactics. This is a Soviet 11D missile on its SM-63-I launcher, better known in the West as the SA-2b. (US DoD)

3

since even a single bomber leaking through the defenses could cause unimaginable damage.

In 1945, Germany was on the verge of deploying revolutionary air defense technology using new guided missiles such as the Wasserfal and the Schmetterling. Early Soviet surface-to-air missile (SAM) design at the NII-88 (*Nauchno-issledovaniy institute*: Scientific Research Institute) was based on German technology. Although many test flights were conducted, these programs came to naught due to the political machinations of the rival Special Bureau No.1 (SB-1) headed by the radar expert Pavel N. Kuksenko. On the staff was Sergei L. Beria, the son of the sinister head of the Soviet secret police, Lavrentiy Beria. They proposed developing an entirely new SAM and in 1951 the rival programs were terminated and their personnel shifted to work on the new Berkut (Golden Eagle) system, an acronym for Beria and Kutepov, the Deputy Director of KB-1. Stalin was alarmed by the reports coming from Korea of the effectiveness of US B-29 bomber attacks, and on August 9, 1950, he ordered that the Berkut be deployed within a year's time to protect Moscow.

The Berkut was an immense undertaking, consisting of 56 missile regiments in two concentric rings around Moscow, each with a massive B-200 radar bunker and 60 launch pads. Missile development was undertaken by the foremost Soviet fighter designer, Semyon Lavochkin, which accounts for his mysterious disappearance from aircraft design in the late 1950s. During the course of the Berkut program, Stalin died and his henchman Lavrentiy Beria was arrested by army officers and shot. In the ensuing purge of Beria supporters, his son was evicted from the design bureau, which was reorganized under S. A. Respletin as KB-1, later becoming better known as the famous Almaz design bureau. Almaz would lead Soviet strategic SAM development for the next half-century. The project was also renamed as S-25 (*Sistema-25*: System-25). The program led to the construction of Moscow's two famous ring-roads, a project that consumed the equivalent of a year's concrete production. The first regiments of the S-25 were deployed, beginning in March 1954, by the PVO-Strany (*Protivovodushnaya Oborona Strany* – National Air Defense Force) and went on permanent alert in June 1956, about four years later than the similar US Army Nike-Ajax SAM. By the time it reached

Seen here at the Khodynka museum are the key components of the first Soviet strategic SAM, the S-25 Berkut with a Lavochkin V-300 missile in the foreground and one of the windmill antennae of the unusual B-200 radar behind.

Even though Dal was canceled, the Lavochkin 5V11 missile was frequently paraded in Red Square, leading NATO to give it the "Griffon" codename, appropriately a mythical beast.

service, the S-25 was already approaching obsolescence due to the rapid changes in aviation technology. The Kremlin considered deploying a cheaper, rail-mobile version, called the S-50, around Leningrad but this was rejected in favor of a much more sophisticated system codenamed Dal. In the event, the Lavochkin Dal program would become mired in its own set of technological and cost problems and was canceled in the early 1960s before becoming operational.

Birth of the S-75

While Moscow and Leningrad might warrant expensive systems, the Kremlin wanted a more economical air defense system to protect other Soviet cities and military bases. This secondary system was designated the S-75 and the program was authorized on November 20, 1953. A design team under Boris Bunkin at the KB-1/Almaz bureau was put in charge of the program. There was some hope of shifting from the low-frequency N-band (10cm) used on the S-25 system to the high-frequency V-band (6cm), but until new N-band magnetrons were completed, the radar program ran on parallel tracks. The low-frequency version of the S-75 system was called SA-75 Dvina and used RSNA-75 radar, while the definitive high-frequency version was called the S-75N Desna and used RSN-75 radar; both versions were named after Russian rivers, a practice that became a tradition with the naming of Soviet strategic SAMs.

Leningrad was supposed to be defended by the more sophisticated Lavochkin Dal system: this shows one of the prototype 5V11 missiles on its massive PPU-476 launcher at the Sary-Shagan test-range.

With Lavochkin busy on both the S-25 missiles and the later Dal missiles, a new organization was created to design the S-75's missiles under one of Lavochkin's deputies, Pyotr Grushin. First known as OKB-2 it is much more famous by its later name, the Fakel (Torch) design bureau, and over the

years it designed most of the Soviet Union's strategic SAMs. A new missile design introduced a two-stage configuration patterned on the experimental ShB-32 missile that offered better performance than a single-stage design such as the V-300 missile of the S-25. The new missile was called *izdeliye* 1D (Item 1D) and was also known by its classified bureau designation of V-750. More sophisticated guidance systems such as semi-active radar were studied but rejected due to time constraints and cost. As a result, the S-75 system used command guidance like the S-25, an approach that later proved to be the Achilles heel of the system in combat use. Flight testing of the 1D missile began in April 1955 at Kapustin Yar.

An SA-75 launch battery consisted of six SM-63-I launchers and an RSNA-75 radar station, typically deployed in a star shape with the radar in the center along with three command shelters and several electrical generator trailers. The RSNA-75 fire control radar had a very narrow beam, so initial target acquisition and tracking was handled by a P-12 Yenisey search radar teamed with a PRV-10 height-finder radar, which passed their data to the RSNA-75 via land-lines, both located on the periphery of the launch site. Each SAM regiment included three SAM batteries plus a technical battalion, and the regiments in turn could be organized into larger formations: brigades, divisions, and PVO-Strany corps.

Progress on the S-75 program was steady enough that the 1956–60 Five-Year Plan envisioned the manufacture of 265 missile batteries and 7,220 V-750 missiles. The SA-75 Dvina system was accepted for service on December 11, 1957. The 1957 production included 30 of the planned 40 launch complexes and 621 of the planned 1,200 missiles.

The evolutionary link between the S-25 and S-75 systems was the experimental ShB-32 missile, which pioneered the two-stage configuration.

This is one of the original Fakel 1D missiles on a prototype launcher during the initial firing trials of the SA-75 system.

The original SA-75 system used the PR-11 transporter-loader semi-trailer, towed by an ATS-59 tractor.

THE SPYPLANE MENACE

On July 4, 1956, Soviet radar detected an aircraft flying deep over Russia at altitudes of 72,000ft (22km), far beyond the reach of Soviet jet interceptors. This was a CIA U-2 spyplane on its maiden overflight of the USSR, and a flight over Moscow followed the next day. Nikita Khrushchev was infuriated and insisted that the new spyplanes had to be shot down. On August 25, 1956, Grushin's design bureau began work on the 11D missile, which increased the maximum altitude from 72,000 to 82,000ft (22km to 25km) with a more powerful rocket engine. Test flights began in late 1957 and were completed in April 1958.

While this work was underway, development of the preferred 6cm band RSN-75 radar was reaching maturity along with the associated 13D missile, which also received the new rocket engine. Production of the new S-75N Desna system began in late 1958 about a year after the baseline V-band SA-75 Dvina, and Desna was accepted for service on May 22, 1959. The 1958 production program called for the manufacture of 130 missile batteries, including 78 Dvina batteries with 950 11D missiles and 52 Desna batteries with 700 13D missiles.

The improved S-75 missile systems had few opportunities to display their high-altitude capabilities. President Eisenhower was worried that sooner or later a U-2 would be shot down over Russia, and so in December 1956 he temporarily halted flights. The CIA attempted to change his mind by deploying an early form of stealth coating for the U-2, which made the aircraft less visible to radar, resulting in the so-called "dirty-bird" U-2s. Although a few more flights were permitted, Eisenhower again restricted the flights when it became apparent that Soviet radar was still tracking the U-2s. From the autumn of 1957 to 1959, only three deep overflights were authorized, one in 1958, and two in 1959; sites heavily protected by the new missile batteries were avoided altogether.

The first success of the S-75 system took place under mysterious circumstances. The Republic of China Air Force (RoCAF) had been staging reconnaissance missions over the People's Republic of China using RF-101 Voodoo aircraft and, in early 1959, the US Air Force transferred three RB-57D high-altitude spyplanes to RoCAF for deep overflights. In 1958 the Soviet Union delivered five SA-75 Dvina batteries, along with a training battery and 62 missiles, to China. Soviet PVO-Strany troops

Each S-75 battery was equipped with a P-12 (NATO: Spoon Rest) surveillance radar to acquire targets for the RSNA-75 fire control radar. The smaller antenna in front is a NRZ-1 identification-friend-or-foe (IFF) interrogator.

helped man the launch sites, which included three around Beijing and the others around major missile and nuclear weapons test sites. On October 7, 1959, one of the Taiwanese RB-57Ds was struck at an altitude of 65,600ft (20km) by a salvo of three V-750 missiles. It was the first time in history that an aircraft was shot down by a SAM, although at the time the feat was attributed to Chinese fighters due to the secrecy of the Chinese S-75 battalions. The first kill in Soviet airspace was claimed on November 16 1959 when an SA-75 battery near Volgograd was credited with shooting down a US WS-416L reconnaissance balloon, although this incident remains unverified.

The Soviet Navy fitted a naval version of the S-75 called the M-2 aboard the cruiser *Dzerzhinskiy* in 1959–62. The M-2 used the massive SM-64 twin-rail launcher with a large drum magazine below decks, which made the system far too cumbersome and it was rejected for further use.

Due to growing political controversy over the Soviet strategic missile program, Eisenhower reluctantly agreed to a resumption of U-2 flights in 1960. The U-2 mission on April 10, 1960, flew near the Tyuratam missile range and passed a number of S-75 batteries that had not been alerted in time. A number of senior Soviet commanders were cashiered when Khrushchev learned of the failure. The next U-2 flight on May Day 1960 became the most infamous. Operation *Grand Slam* was piloted by Francis Gary Powers and flew from Pakistan towards Tyuratam and the Sary-shagan anti-ballistic missile proving ground. The PVO-Strany managed to track the U-2 almost continuously from the Soviet-Afghan border, and more than a dozen fighter aircraft were sent up to intercept it, including one attempt to ram it using a new Su-9 interceptor. The CIA had a very incomplete picture of the density of air defenses in the Urals, and the Sverdlovsk area had a heavy concentration of missile defenses since it was the center of the Soviet nuclear weapons industry. The new production line at the Kalinnin plant in the city

To reach the U-2's high cruising altitude, a more powerful sustainer engine for the new Fakel 11D missile was needed, the Isayev S.711V seen to the left. The engine to the right is the S2.270-A1 developed for later versions.

had recently begun to deliver the new 13D missile to local SAM batteries. In the vicinity of Sverdlovsk, a PVO-Strany regiment newly equipped with the latest S-75N Desna engaged the U-2 from two of its batteries. A 13D missile from the battery, commanded by Maj Mikhail Voronov, scored a near miss behind the U-2 at around around 67,000ft (20.5km) at 0853 hours, which shattered the control surfaces of the U-2 and caused it to spiral out of control. Powers managed to escape the doomed aircraft by parachute, and shortly afterwards the U-2 was hit by another missile,

The 11D missile became the standard export variant, and one is seen here on display at the Polish Army Museum in Warsaw on its SM-63 launcher.

The SA-75M Dvina system introduced the newer PR-11A transporter-loader semi-trailer, which was towed by a ZIL-151V truck. Here, a Romanian crew is seen reloading an 11D missile on an SM-63-I launcher.

which broke it apart. The shoot-down of the U-2 and capture of Powers was a major embarrassment for the Eisenhower administration and led Eisenhower to forbid any further flights over the Soviet Union by the U-2, a ban which was later extended to its supersonic follow-on, the SR-71. However, overflights did continue in other regions including China, North Korea, and the Middle East. By this time, new sources of overhead photography of the USSR were becoming available, the Corona spy satellites, which reduced the need for provocative overflights.

OPERATION *ANADYR*: THE CUBAN MISSILE CRISIS

By 1962, there was indeed a missile gap, but it was not the United States that was behind. The Soviet R-7 intercontinental missile program had proven to be a technological dead-end and it took years before the next-generation R-16 missile was deployed in significant numbers. As a short-cut, Khrushchev decided to deploy existing intermediate-range nuclear-armed ballistic missiles in Cuba, where they could reach most of the United States. Operation *Anadyr* also involved the PVO-Strany to

The regimental technical battalion maintained additional missiles in these sealed containers carried on a semi-trailer.

To commemorate the shoot-down of Powers' U-2, this Fakel 13D missile on its SM-63 launcher was placed outside the Sverdlovsk military museum, where the remains of the U-2 are on display.

defend the ballistic missile sites. The PVO-Strany forces in Cuba were commanded by GenLt S. N. Grechko and consisted of the 10th and 11th Air Defense Missile Divisions from the Volga PVO-Strany Military District, each with three missile regiments, totaling some 144 SAM launchers of the newer S-75 Desna version. The S-75 missile batteries began arriving in Cuba in the final week of July, and construction of the SAM sites took place from August to September 1962.

The sudden upsurge in Soviet activity in Cuba led to the dispatch of a CIA U-2 on August 29, which detected the first eight SA-2 sites. CIA Director John McCone was convinced that the USSR would only deploy such a new and sophisticated system if they were trying to protect something especially valuable such as ballistic missiles. The discovery of the SA-2 sites forced the Kennedy administration to be more wary of sending U-2s over Cuba, but at the same time increased the pressure for more frequent coverage. The hurricane season hampered the reconnaissance missions and so the first clear evidence of the deployment of R-14 (SS-4) intermediate range ballistic missiles was not acquired until a U-2 flight on October 14. The ensuing crisis brought the USA and USSR to the brink of nuclear war.

Grechko had been instructed to use the S-75 batteries only in the event of hostilities or a direct attack. In frustration at the Soviet inaction in response to the overflights, on October 26 Castro ordered his anti-aircraft units to engage low-flying US reconnaissance aircraft even though the Cuban guns could not reach the U-2. It seemed unlikely that the US would overlook this act, and the Soviets believed that war was imminent. On October 27, when another U-2 was spotted, Grechko attempted to reach the commander of the Group of Soviet Forces-Cuba for permission to engage. After being unable to do so, he ordered the 507th Air Defense Missile Regiment to shoot down the U-2, based on his mistaken presumption that war was inevitable. The U-2 was engaged by the 4th Battery, commanded by LtCol I. M. Gerchenov and stationed near Victoria-de-las-Tunas. The aircraft was hit with a salvo of three missiles around 1019hrs, killing the pilot, USAF Maj Rudolph Anderson. This incident almost precipitated a nuclear war.

Stunned by the news, Khrushchev realized that his original instructions had not been explicit enough and a message was sent to Grechko warning "You were hasty" and insisting on greater caution. Likewise, on the US side, there was recognition that the situation was spiraling out of control. Calmer reasoning prevailed, and during the course of secret negotiations over the next few days, the crisis began to subside. The eventual settlement included the removal of the Soviet ballistic missiles from Cuba, and without the missiles to protect, most of the S-75 batteries were withdrawn as well. A total of 24 S-75 combat and six training launchers were left behind for the Cuban forces in 1963. Details of the U-2 shoot-down were a closely guarded secret for many years and a number of myths circulated around the incident. Castro made the preposterous claim that he had ordered the SAM attack, and there were fanciful stories in the US press about how Cuban troops had stormed a Soviet SAM battery, and launched the missile that downed the U-2.

As the Cuban missile crisis captured world attention, other battles between the U-2 and the S-75 went almost unnoticed. While the US government was increasingly reluctant to operate the U-2 in deep- penetration

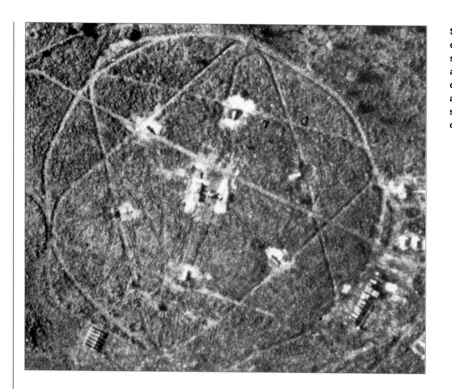

Soviet attempts to hide missile deployment in Cuba in the summer of 1962 were given away by the characteristic deployment pattern of the associated S-75 systems, as seen in this U-2 photo taken over Cuba. (US DoD)

missions over the Soviet Union and China, the RoCAF was willing to take up the China mission. As a result, the US began transferring U-2s to Taiwan and missions began in 1962. The first RoCAF U-2 was shot down over Nachang on September 9, 1962, and at least 11 RoCAF U-2s were lost between 1962 and 1970, mostly victims of the S-75 missile system. The S-75 was also used in small numbers by India during the 1965 war with Pakistan.

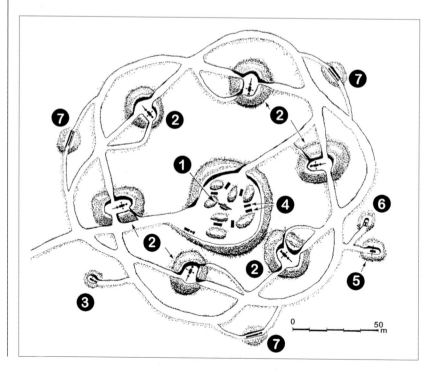

Each S-75 battery was usually deployed in a star-shape pattern, with the principal equipment protected in earthen berms. At the center is the RSN-75 (Fan Song) radar (1) along with associated command trailers and generators (4), which are linked to the rest of the regiment via a Mercury Grass communication vehicle (3). The six SM-63 launchers (2) are around the command site. The P-12 search radar (5) provides the initial target acquisition and alongside is a generator trailer (6). Each battery site is supported by three PR-11 missile transporter-loaders (7) with spare missiles.

DEEP MODERNIZATION

The S-75M Volkhov

When the S-75 system was taken to mass production in 1957, there was already some recognition of the need for greater range and altitude to deal with future threats beyond the U-2. One option was to develop an entirely new system, the S-175. However, a new system would take time and because so much money had already been invested in the S-75, the PVO-Strany decided instead on a deep modernization of the existing S-75. Development of the S-75M Volkhov system was authorized on June 4, 1958, and aimed at increasing system performance against faster targets at longer ranges. Two different missiles were considered for the new version, items 17D and 20D.

The 17D was a fundamentally different approach to missile propulsion, using a ram-jet engine for the sustainer stage rather than a liquid-fuel rocket. The ram-jet engine removed the need for the oxidizer that made up about two-thirds of the propellant weight in the normal version. It was such a radical departure from the previous designs that its development took much longer than the 20D. The first flight test did not take place until January 23, 1960, after the rival 20D had already been accepted for the S-75M system. About 40 test flights were conducted through the summer of 1962 and led to more sophisticated ram-jet derivatives such as the 19D and 22D.

The 20D was similar in appearance to the previous S-75 missiles, but nearly all the internal components were redesigned and replaced. Since the Fakel bureau was so busy with newer SAM systems, development was handed over to a small affiliated engineering bureau headed by V. V. Kolyaskin, which was located at the lead production facility, the Avangard Plant in Moscow. A significant rationale for the new program was to improve tracking performance in the presence of hostile radar jamming. The new substantially modernized RSN-75V radar (NATO: Fan Song E)

The Fakel 22D missile was yet another attempt to extend the range of the S-75 system, this time by adding a set of four ram-jet sustainers around the core liquid-fuel rocket engine.

was able to track up to six targets simultaneously and it featured the more powerful Biser-M magnetron and a pair of new pencil-beam tracking antennae above the cabin. The radar's performance was improved with a moving-target-indicator to deal with chaff, and optional manual and mixed manual/automatic tracking modes for operations when electronic jamming was present. The S-75M Volkhov system was accepted for service on April 20, 1961, but the first batteries did not deploy with the PVO-Strany until 1962 due to lingering bottlenecks in the factories. By 1967, production had reached about 68,000 S-75 missiles.

There was some recognition in the PVO-Strany that the conventionally armed S-75 system did not provide a leak-proof defense against bomber attack. This led to the development of the nuclear-armed 15D missile, which could be fired by the batteries of the S-75M Volkhov system. The missile was similar to the 20D, except that it had a more bulbous nose to house the new nuclear warhead, and it had redundant flight controls for higher reliability. To ensure greater precision when using a nuclear-armed missile, a new range-finding radar, the RD-75 Amazonka, was deployed with the nuclear batteries. It was accepted for service on May 15, 1964.

By 1961, the PVO-Strany had deployed 435 S-75 batteries throughout the USSR, and deployment reached a peak in 1969 with some 800 battery sites. In the summer of 1959, the S-75 air defense umbrella was extended westward with the first deployment of Soviet batteries in East Germany. In 1960 Khrushchev informed the leaders of the other Warsaw Pact countries that they would be honored to purchase the new S-75 air defense systems, which would be installed on a crash basis within three months. Transfer of missiles to the other Warsaw Pact armies began in 1961, with priority going to the first-tier armies of Poland, Czechoslovakia, and East Germany. Although the Warsaw Pact countries began with the SA-75 Dvina system, the high cost of the program forced them to stretch out their acquisition so that they eventually acquired the more modern S-75 Volkhov system in the late 1960s. So, for example, East Germany acquired eight batteries of the SA-75 Dvina and 29 batteries of the S-75 Volkhov.

The Volkhov system introduced the improved SM-90 launcher, which had a more durable flame deflector and an improved tracker drive. This view of a Polish launcher shows the characteristic features of the 20D missile such as the forward dielectric band and the four antenna strakes behind the nose fins.

The next generation: S-125 and S-200

Like many Cold War weapons, the S-75 was developed in haste and was plagued by a number of shortcomings. It had poor performance at low altitudes and the U-2 overflights displayed its limitations against high-altitude targets as well. The US was likely to introduce new supersonic bombers and spyplanes beyond the effective envelope of the S-75. Some of these problems were partially addressed by the upgrades mentioned earlier, but a more thorough approach was to develop a pair of new missile systems to supplement the S-75 – the low-altitude S-125 Neva (NATO: SA-3 Goa) and the high-altitude S-200 Angara (NATO: SA-5 Gammon). The S-125 was accepted for service in June 1961 and was deployed by

The new Almaz RSN-75V (Fan Song E) radar for the Volkhov system introduced a pair of new parabolic antennae to add a "lobe-on-receive-only" (LORO) mode to help frustrate the radar warning receivers on targeted aircraft.

the PVO-Strany alongside the S-75 regiments to deepen the low-altitude coverage. An export version, the S-125 Pechora, was widely sold around the world and first saw combat in 1970 over Egypt.

The S-200 Angara was a much greater technological challenge and was not accepted for service until February 1967. By this time, the focus of intercontinental nuclear strike forces had shifted from bombers to intercontinental ballistic missiles, but the S-200 program went ahead anyway, if only as an insurance policy against the overflights of the new SR-71 Blackbird spyplane. An export version, the S-200VE Vega-E, was developed in the 1980s and exported in modest numbers to the Warsaw Pact countries as well as to Syria, Libya, Iran, and North Korea.

Both the S-125 and S-200 supplemented the S-75 rather than replaced it. However, the growing number of PVO-Strany regiments with these new missile systems led to the gradual decline in the number of S-75 regiments, from their peak in 1968 with some 800 battery sites to about 465 battery sites in the USSR a decade later. The final replacement for the S-75 was the new S-300P Volkhov (NATO: SA-10 Grumble) which was accepted for service in 1981. This is the Russian equivalent of the US Army's Patriot and is widely used by Russia, as well as by a number of export customers including China, and some of the former Soviet republics and Warsaw Pact countries.

Parallel to the 20D missile with its V-88 conventional warhead, Avangard also developed the 15D missile with a larger nosecone to accommodate a nuclear warhead. A 15D missile is seen here being carried on a PR-11B transporter-loader semi-trailer, towed by a ZiL-131 tractor truck. (US DoD)

THE FLYING TELEPHONE POLE IN VIETNAM

Even though the S-75 had been developed for strategic air defense of the Soviet Union against long-range bombers, its greatest fame came from its use in Vietnam against tactical strike aircraft. Due to increasing US air raids, in July 1965 the Soviet government agreed to provide air defense missiles to North Vietnam. Although the new S-125 system was better suited to the tactical requirements of the air campaign, the Soviet Union was only willing to provide the first-generation SA-75 Dvina. Vietnamese personnel were dispatched to the Soviet Union for training, and ten PVO-Strany training centers were formed in North Vietnam, to become the core of new SAM regiments. Since it would take some time for the Vietnamese crews to become proficient, the PVO-Strany began to dispatch missile crews from the Moscow and Baku PVO-Strany districts, headed by GenMaj Grigoriy A. Belov. From April 1965 to May 1967, a total of 2,266 Soviet SAM personnel were deployed to Vietnam. In total, some 10,900 Soviet military personnel and 6,214 civilian technicians served in Vietnam during the war, primarily with the air defense force, and at least four were killed in combat. The first few Vietnamese SAM regiments were based around a Soviet cadre; for example the 274th Missile Regiment was based around the Soviet 260th SAM Regiment from Bryansk with Soviet officers commanding the regiment, its four launch batteries, and its associated technical battalion. By 1967–68, Vietnamese officers gradually took over regimental command, with a Soviet officer delegated as a technical advisor, although some Soviet officers remained as battery commanders through the late 1960s.

The first S-75 Dvina regiment in combat was the 236th Air Defense Regiment commanded by Col M. Tsygankov with its first two launch battalions in

One of the contenders for the Volkhov modernization program was Fakel's 17D missile, which is easily distinguishable by the thicker mid-fuselage area, widened to accommodate a ram-jet sustainer.

The poor performance of the S-75 at low altitude and short range led to the development of the complementary S-125 Neva system. This is an example of the later S-125M Neva-M with four 5V27 (V-601) missiles on the four-rail 5P73 launcher; the earlier system used the two-rail 5P71 launcher.

the Hanoi area. On July 24, 1965, the 63rd and 64th batteries of the 236th SAM Regiment hit a formation of F-4C Phantom fighter bombers of the USAF 47th Tactical Fighter Squadron northwest of Hanoi, shooting down a single aircraft. A second Dvina unit, the 238th Missile Regiment (Col N. V. Bazhenov), became operational in the autumn, the 261st commanded by Col K. V. Zavadskiy in February 1966, and the 274th commanded by Col V. V. Fedorov later in 1966.

The initial USAF efforts to deal with the SA-2 sites were not successful. The missions against the SAM sites were called Operation *Iron Hand*, a pioneering effort in SEAD (suppression of enemy air defenses). Since the Fan Song radar had a dead zone at low altitude where it was blind, the first *Iron Hand* attack on July 27, 1965, involved a low-altitude attack by 54 F-105 fighter bombers. However, the 236th Missile Regiment anticipated an attack, and so moved the SAM batteries involved, replacing them with dummies and deploying about 120 anti-aircraft guns around the area. When the F-105s arrived, they were blasted by numerous anti-aircraft guns, losing six F-105s and an RF-101 Voodoo reconnaissance aircraft. After a Navy A-4E was lost to an SA-2 on August 11, a similar Navy attack was launched, losing five more aircraft to anti-aircraft guns without hitting the SAM sites. More sophisticated approaches were tried, such as Operation *Left Hook* on August 21, which launched an unmanned BQM-34 Firebee drone as bait to listen for Fan Song signals. On the first try, the Soviets did not take the bait, and on the second try, the triangulation effort was not accurate enough to locate the radar. In the month from August 12 to September 14, some 388 *Iron Hand* missions were flown without success due to the mobility of the missile batteries, their excellent camouflage, and heavy anti-aircraft gun defenses around the sites.

Having failed to blunt the SA-2 using brute force, the US began to turn to electronic warfare. The first step was to use electronic intelligence (ELINT) aircraft, such as the EB-66C, to monitor the various signals from the SA-2 radars, to develop an understanding of how they worked and their potential vulnerabilities. The CIA launched Firebee drones into SAM areas with signal repeaters that transmitted the signals picked up by the drone's antennae back to the DC-130 mother ship. A mission on February 13, 1966, hit the mother lode, finally acquiring the long-mysterious command uplink and downlink signals. The CIA eventually managed to purchase a Fan Song radar from Indonesia.

The SA-2 system was vulnerable to electronic counter-measures (ECM) at several key nodes of its "kill chain." The SAM regiment began operations by acquiring a target using P-15 early warning radars, which then handed the target over to the battery's own P-12 search radar. These radars were needed since the Fan Song had a very narrow ten-degree surveillance sector, so jamming or otherwise interfering with acquisition, and tracking radars would interrupt the kill chain. Once the Fan Song began tracking the target, it emitted a very distinctive radar signal that could be picked up by the aircraft's radar warning receiver (RWR). Evasive maneuvers could often break the Fan Song's automatic tracking, and by the time the Fan Song reacquired the fighter 45 seconds later, the aircraft could be out of range. Later RWR sets could also distinguish between the initial tracking signal of the Fan Song and its transition to firing mode. This often proved to be the most critical phase of all, since the missile or radar could often be evaded if the pilot was warned soon enough. A critical deficiency of the SA-2 missile was that it had never been designed to engage maneuverable tactical aircraft at low altitudes. The control surfaces on the missile were relatively small, and while the rocket engine was burning the high speed of the missile limited its maneuvering capability as well. After the rocket engine burned out, the SA-2 missile faced a second problem since it was coasting, and every maneuver burned off much of its speed to the point at which it could not maneuver at all. If pilots spotted the "flying telephone-pole" in time they could outmaneuver it.

The US Air Force and US Navy set about attacking all the various nodes of this kill chain in order to reduce the threat of the SA-2. Deception jamming pods were fitted to strike aircraft, which created false range information for the Fan Song operators. The USAF discovered that flying four F-105s equipped with jammers in tight formation amplified their effectiveness, and these tactics were introduced in September 1966. Another solution was to mount more powerful equipment on a larger aircraft which could accompany a strike package and shield the entire group using powerful deception jammers, as well as powerful noise jammers that rendered the SAM radars ineffective by simply overwhelming

To deal with future supersonic high-altitude threats such as the SR-71 reconnaissance aircraft and B-70 bomber, the S-200 Angara (SA-5 Gammon) system was accepted for service in 1967. This is a Fakel 5V21 (V-860) missile on its single-rail 5P72 launcher.

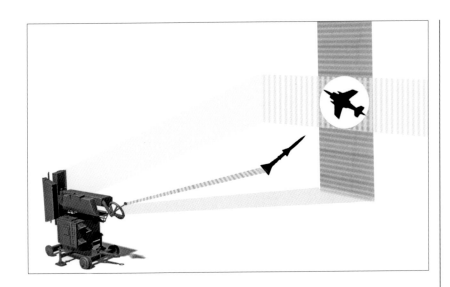

The RSNA-75 (Fan Song B) radar used electro-mechanical scanning technology, emitting a pair of beams from its two perpendicular antennae, which formed a cross-shaped pattern to determine the height and azimuth of the target. The round antenna on the right side of the array transmitted command signals to the missile, guiding it towards the target.

them with so much radio noise that they could not detect the radio echo of their own radar. An important change in the *Iron Hand* operations was the development of modified strike aircraft dedicated to hunting and destroying SAM sites, codenamed Wild Weasels. The F-105 Wild Weasel introduced an important innovation, the AGM-45 Shrike anti-radar missile (ARM) that homed in on the Fan Song's own radar signal. Besides destroying many Fan Song radars, the Shrikes also were useful to blind the SAM sites during missions, since Fan Song crews turned off their radar if they realized a Shrike was on the way. In March 1968, the Shrike was joined by the new and larger AGM-78 Standard ARM which could memorize the location of the Fan Song site and so strike it even if the radar was turned off. The Shrike and Standard ARM missiles comprised a relatively small proportion of the many tons of bombs and unguided rockets used to attack the SAM sites, but they were by far the most effective weapon for this mission, accounting for 46 percent of the SA-2 batteries knocked out during the Vietnam war.

The North Vietnamese were deeply alarmed by the new electronic warfare tactics, which substantially degraded SA-2 performance. The Soviet PVO-Strany specialists estimated that it took one to two missiles per kill in 1965, but three to four in 1966. However, since Soviet and Vietnamese kill claims were about seven times higher than actual losses, the figures were closer to ten missiles in 1965 and 25 missiles-per-kill in 1966. Teams from the Soviet design bureaus and production plants were stationed in Hanoi to study the new tactics and suggest missile improvements. The new US tactical innovations were so effective that the Vietnamese were forced to place greater emphasis on fighter aircraft to defend Hanoi, and the Vietnam People's Air Force (VPAF) lost half of its fighter pilots in the March–June 1967 dogfights.

The Soviet PVO-Strany specialists instructed the Vietnamese radar operators to reduce the time that the Fan Song radar transmitted, making it less visible to the Wild Weasels. However, turning off the radar often backfired since once switched back on again, it took more than a minute for the radar to warm up to full power, by which time the US aircraft were usually gone. Instead of switching the radar off, Soviet engineers modified existing maintenance equipment to allow the Fan

The 11D missile used in Vietnam had two sets of strip antenna on the nose, the forward set for the radio proximity fuze, and the aft set for receiving command guidance signals.

Song operator to switch the transmitter into a "dummy load," which left the radar at full power but not transmitting. As a result, the radar could wait in ambush until the last possible moment, and then switch from dummy load to transmit mode to ambush an unsuspecting fighter. The 236th Missile Regiment also pioneered a technique of switching from automatic to manual tracking, called "three-point" guidance, when under intense electronic jamming, scoring a first victory using this tactic on August 12, 1967.

In spite of these innovations, US electronic warfare techniques continued to degrade the effectiveness of the missile regiments. In the August 1967 fighting over Hanoi, 66 percent of all SA-2 missiles lost control, and more than 6 percent lost control so near the ground that they impacted near the city, causing considerable death and destruction. The missile regiments became so desperate during the October 1967 air battles over Hanoi that they began using untested track-on-jam tactics, attempting to steer the missile using the aircraft's own jamming signals. Although 22 aircraft were claimed by SAM batteries during the intense October 24–27 air battles, in fact only five were lost. Between November 17 and 19 the US lost eight more planes to the improved SA-2 tactics and the Vietnamese were convinced that the jammer problem had been solved. Instead, the tide turned again in favor of the jammers. New QRC-160-8 jamming pods were specifically directed to overwhelm the command uplink between the radar and the missile and these were deployed in December 1967 with dramatic results. On December 14, 1967, during air battles over Hanoi, every single SA-2 launched crashed shortly after launch. On December 15, 1967, the 236th Missile Regiment, Vietnam's most experienced, fired eight missiles and all but one crashed; another regiment fired 29 missiles and 11 immediately went out of control. The same situation occurred on the following three days of

One of the few innovations provided to the Vietnamese was the RSN-75V2 (Fan Song F) radar upgrade, which added the small "bird house" above the horizontal antenna, where two crewmen could track and guide the missile optically in intense electronic jamming conditions.

December before the monsoon season arrived, which curtailed air attacks. On February 14, 1968, the 61st Battery, 236th Missile Regiment shot down an F-105 and its QRC-160-8 pod was recovered. This led to a Soviet program to modify the V-750's FR-15 transponder beacon. However, President Johnson's decision to halt further air attacks north of the 20th parallel after March 31, 1968, brought a halt to the missile war for more than four years.

Applying the lessons: *Linebacker II*

In October 1966, the Soviet government dispatched a special military-industrial delegation to Vietnam, led by the head of the PVO-Strany, Gen P. F. Batitskiy, to examine the results of the air campaign and to recommend future directions for air defense missile development, including potential improvements to the S-75 system. As an interim step, improved versions of the 11D missile in use by the Vietnamese were sent with the modified transponder beacon. The RSNA-75 radar was modified by adding a "bird house" over the horizontal antenna, where a pair of operators could optically track the missile when electronic jamming prevented normal operations. This improvement allowed the missile to be fired under intense electronic warfare conditions, but was dependent on manual guidance and was vulnerable to cloudy weather conditions.

The Vietnamese were using the first-generation SA-75MK Dvina version of the S-75 system, and the Batitskiy commission recommended that the most recent version, the S-75M1 Volkhov should also undergo thorough modernization to cope with the new electronic warfare environment. This system already had some electronic counter-measure features incorporated, but the Vietnam lessons were applied to further improvements in the new RSN-75V2 radar and the Avangard 5Ya23 missile. The resulting

S-75M2 Volkhov system was accepted for service in April 1971. There was a parallel effort to deploy a nuclear-armed version, the S-75M3 with the 5V29 missile, which was accepted for service in April 1975 and deployed in 1977.

However, the Vietnamese did not benefit from the Volkhov-M2 improvements as the Soviet Union was unwilling to supply it with more modern systems than the modestly upgraded Dvina systems. China and the USSR had nearly gone to war in 1968 over border disputes and the PVO-Strany was concerned that any missile technology that went to Vietnam would fall into Chinese hands. The USSR had agreed to sell Vietnam the new S-125 system in 1970, but the two new regiments were still training on the system in late 1972 when the next major phase of the Vietnam air war broke out.

The US ban on air attacks remained in effect in the Hanoi and Haiphong areas, but as a result of the 1972 North Vietnamese offensive the air campaign was resumed along the Demilitarized Zone (DMZ). In November 1972, SA-2 batteries were deployed in the area and on the night of November 22, 1972, managed to shoot down a B-52D bomber, the first such loss of the war. With the peace negotiations in Paris stalled, in mid-December 1972 President Nixon ordered the start of Operation *Linebacker II*, a renewed bombing offensive against Hanoi and Haiphong aimed at forcing North Vietnam to sign a peace treaty that would extricate the US from the war. Until this operation, B-52 bombers had been ordered to abort any missions where SA-2 missiles were detected, but this policy changed for these final raids, and the bomber crews were ordered to press home the attacks regardless of the missile threat. By this stage of the war, the B-52 fleet had been heavily modified with electronic warfare equipment: all of the B-52D fleet and about half the B-52G fleet had been upgraded with the Phase V ECM suite. Unfortunately, half the B-52G fleet was only fitted with the Phase III suite, giving them less protection against the SA-2. In addition, the USAF did not appreciate that the Soviets had modified the SA-2 missile based on the lessons from the 1967 campaign, and in particular had replaced the FR-15 downlink transponder on the missile, which made command link jammers ineffective.

The North Vietnamese had problems of their own. At the time, the missile inventory stood at about 1,500 SA-2 missiles but about 40 percent were sidelined with technical problems. Missile inventories near Hanoi were low because many missiles had been sent south to support the operations there. Since the *Linebacker II* missions would be flown at night, the new optical adjunct on the Fan Song was useless, and the North Vietnamese crews would be forced to use the tricky "three-point" manual guidance tactic.

The first B-52 attacks on the night of December 18, 1972, came as a great shock to Hanoi. The amount of jamming stunned the SAM crews,

The last major version of the SA-2 missile was the Avangard 5Ya23 for the S-75M2 Volkhov system. This variant can be distinguished by the gray dielectric band forward of the nose fins, and its lacking of the antenna strakes farther behind that were present on the earlier 20D missile.

but the chaff clouds dropped to shield the bombers from the Fan Songs were dispersed by the wind. The bombers passed over the SAM batteries where the radars could burn through the jamming for a few moments, and more critically when the big bombers made their post-target-turn, their jammers were ineffective and they became visible to the radars. Losses that night included three B-52 bombers shot down and two damaged. Strategic Air Command (SAC) planners had staggered the waves of attacks at four-hour intervals, which allowed the SAM batteries to replenish their launchers. These poor tactics were due to SAC concerns about aerial collisions amongst the big bombers on night missions.

The second raid against Hanoi on the night of December 20 was a disaster. The 361st Air Defense Division shifted their battery deployments to the routes used by the B-52 bombers during the first night, and to their amazement, the B-52s flew the same routes. The one-day lull had given the batteries time to practice new tactics to exploit the period of radar burn-through and the post-target-turn radar visibility. To soak up the Shrike anti-radar missiles from accompanying Wild Weasels, the Hanoi SAM batteries turned on their Fan Songs momentarily, then turned them off once the Shrikes were fired, making them "go stupid." The first wave, which included a significant number of poorly protected B-52Gs, lost three bombers to the SAMs. In total, six B-52 bombers were lost that night and the Vietnamese felt so confident with the results that they walked out of the Paris negotiations the next day. The bombers switched to other targets for the next few nights while changes were made to tactics, and the North Vietnamese shifted the 363rd Air Defense Division from Haiphong to reinforce the capital.

SA-2 ENGAGEMENTS DURING *LINEBACKER II*, DECEMBER 18–29, 1972

Date*	18	19	20	21	22**	26	26**	27	28	29	Total
S-75 batteries active	9	10	10	9	5	13	5	12	11	8	9.2 (avg.)
Engagements	36	12	20	10	11	24	6	20	5	3	147
Missiles launched	68	20	34	17	20	45	12	36	8	6	266
Aircraft claimed (B-52/other)	3/2	2	7/1	3	2	6	1/2	4	2	1	31/25
B-52s shot down	3	0	6	2	0	1	0	2	0	0	14
B-52s seriously damaged	2	1	1	0	0	1	0	0	0	0	5

*Mission start date; includes subsequent waves into the early hours of the following morning
**Engagements over Haiphong

When the B-52 bombers returned to Hanoi on the night of December 26, the tactics had been completely changed. Instead of coming in waves an hour apart along the same dangerous routes, the entire mission was staged in about 20 minutes with bombers coming from numerous directions, and most post-target-turns were eliminated. These tactics also permitted the creation of dense and effective chaff clouds to blind the Fan Songs, aided by the fact that all the bombers were the better protected B-52Ds. The attack was a complete success for the US, with over 2,000 tons (1,814 tonnes) of bombs dropped. Even though there were far more launchers and missiles available than on previous nights, the number of missile engagements was small compared to the number of bombers, due to the effectiveness of the jamming, and most missiles

S-75 COMBAT PERFORMANCE IN VIETNAM AIR WAR

	1965	1966	1967	1968	1969	1970	1971	1972	1973	Total
Engagement vs. aircraft	67	348	1,104	220	10	14	266	1,135	64	3,228
Engagement vs. RPV	7	28	34	100	140	21	16	20	0	366
Total engagements	74	376	1,138	320	150	35	282	1,155	64	3,594
Missiles fired at aircraft	109	590	1,894	376	16	23	136	2,032	72	5,248
Missiles fired at RPV	14	59	58	155	191	27	25	27	0	556
Total missiles fired	123	649	1,952	531	207	50	161	2,059	72	5,804
Aircraft claimed	87	186	411	96	2	2	32	415	62	1,293
RPV claimed	6	17	24	23	41	7	6	6	0	130
Total aircraft/ RPV claimed	93	203	435	119	43	9	38	421	62	1,423
Actual aircraft losses	11	34	60	11	0	0	5	73	3	197
System effectiveness vs. aircraft (%)	16.4	9.7	5.4	20.0	-	-	1.9	6.4	4.6	6.1
Missiles per aircraft kill	9.9	17.3	31.6	34.2	-	-	27.2	27.8	24.0	26.6

were wasted. Only a single B-52 was lost over Hanoi and a second bomber was seriously damaged, and crashed while landing in Thailand. In spite of the exaggerated kill claims of the SAM batteries, the North Vietnamese government the next day sent a message to Washington that they were willing to reopen treaty negotiations. The attacks continued over the next few nights on a reduced scale, including several missions to destroy known SAM supply centers. SA-2 launches dropped dramatically in number due to dwindling supplies. With the North Vietnamese forced back to the treaty negotiations, the missions over Hanoi were called off on December 31, ending *Linebacker II*.

During the war, the Soviet Union supplied North Vietnam with 95 combat batteries of the SA-75 Dvina system, of which 56 were destroyed in combat, leaving 39 functioning batteries at the end of the war. In addition, a total of 7,658 V-750 missiles of various versions were supplied, of which 852 remained at the end of the war. A total of 5,804 missiles

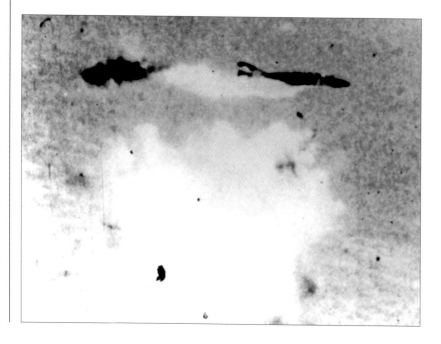

A dramatic view as an 11D missile explodes under a USAF RF-4 Phantom over the Red River area of Vietnam in 1971. The missile used a proximity fuze that detonated the warhead when its trajectory was nearest the target. (USAF)

A: The SA-2 missile

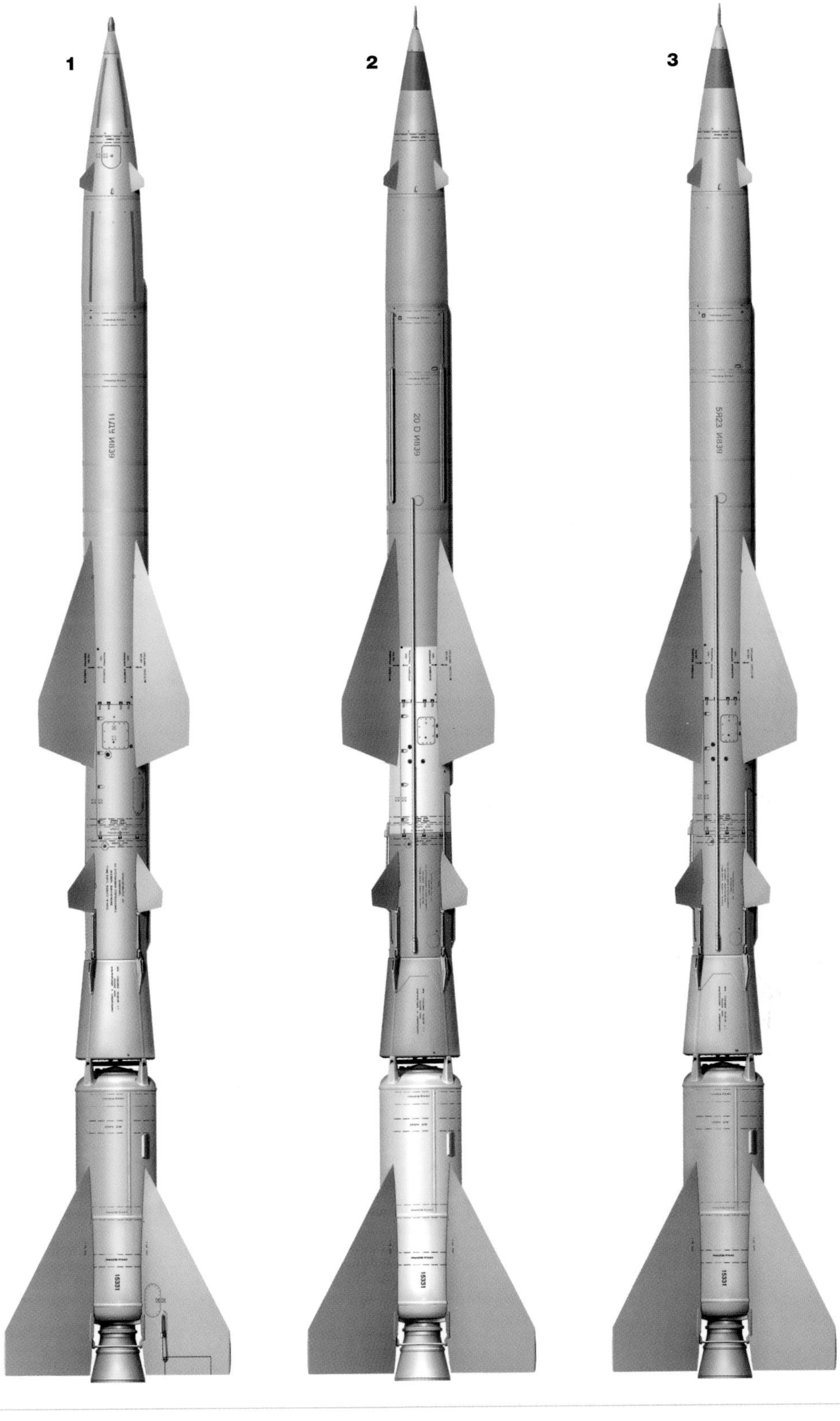

1

2

3

A

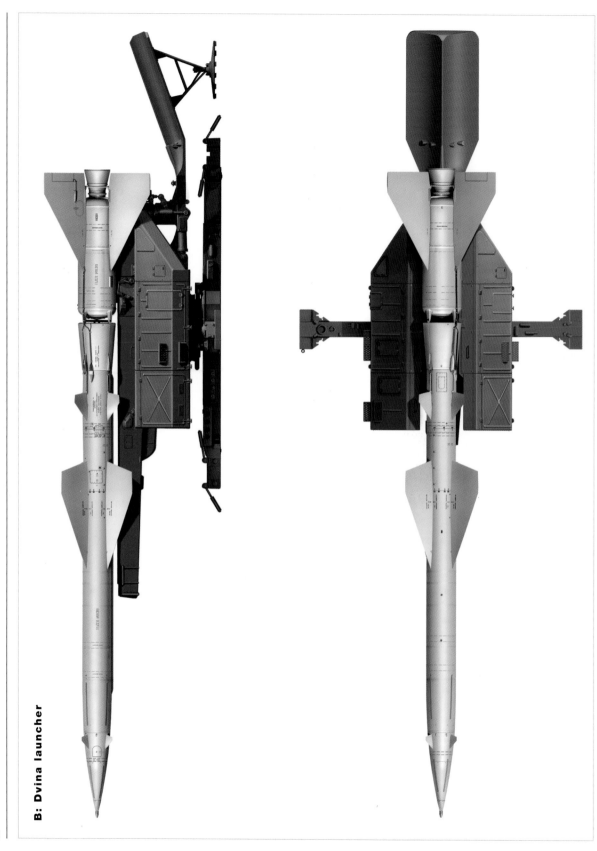

B: Dvina launcher

C: Operation *Grand Slam*: U-2 over Sverdlovsk, May 1, 1960

c

D: DVINA SYSTEM

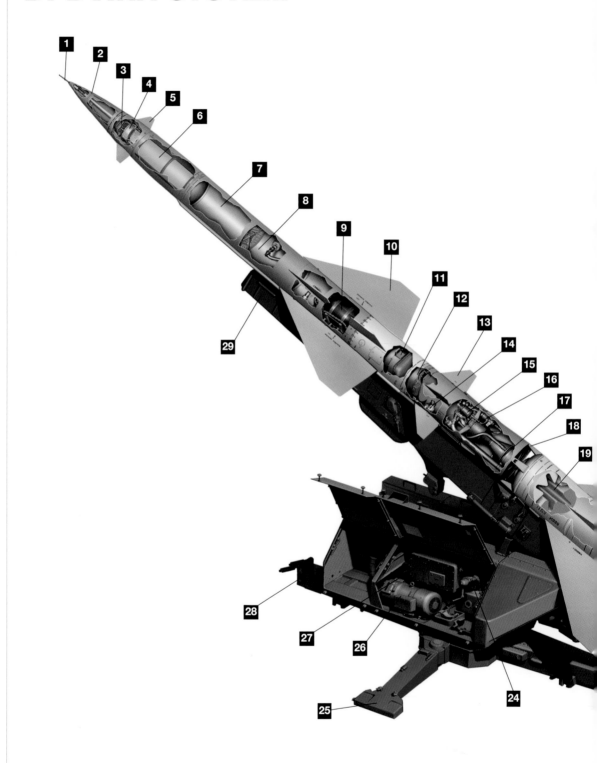

1 Pitot tube
2 Antenna for radio proximity fuze
3 FR-15 Shmel radio proximity fuze
4 Safe and arming device
5 Forward canard stability fin
6 High-explosive fragmentation warhead
7 TG-02 fuel tank
8 AK-20F oxidizer tank
9 Air pressure bottle for fuel system
10 Fixed mid-body stabilization fin
11 Autopilot
12 Radio command receiver
13 Steering fin
14 Fin actuating servo
15 Rocket engine turbo-pump
16 S2.711V rocket engine
17 Rocket engine exhaust chamber
18 Radio command antenna
19 PRD-18 solid fuel rocket booster
20 Booster stabilization fin
21 Booster exhaust chamber
22 Rocket exhaust deflector
23 Exhaust deflector stability pad
24 Manual back-up for traverse
25 Folding outrigger for cruciform base
26 Electric motor for elevation/traverse system
27 Fuse box for launcher electrical system
28 Main cruciform base for SM-63-I launcher
29 Launch rail for SM-63-I launcher

SPECIFICATIONS

System Data:

System design	Almaz Design Bureau (KB-1)
System designation	SA-75M Dvina
Missile designation	11D (V-750V)
Launcher designation	SM-63-I
US/NATO designation	SA-2b Guideline Mod 1
Fire control radar	RSNA-75M (Fan Song B)
System effectiveness	80% probability of kill with 3-missile salvo (theoretical)

Missile Data:

Design	Fakel Design Bureau (OKB-2)
Length	10.726m (35.1ft)
Fuselage diameter	0.5m (1.6ft)
Booster diameter	0.65m (2.1ft)
Max span	2.5m (8.2ft)
Max speed	Mach 3
Weight	2,287kg (5,040lb)
Warhead	19kg (420lb) high-explosive fragmentation with FR-15 Shmel radio proximity fuze
Booster motor	Kartukov PRD-18 solid rocket, 27–50 metric ton thrust; 3–5 second burn-time
Sustainer engine	Isayev S2.711V liquid fuel rocket
Engine performance	3,100kg thrust; 25s burn-time; 45.1kg/cubic cm chamber pressure
Engine propellants	TG-02 fuel, AK-20F oxidizer, OT-155 for engine turbo-pump
Maximum effective range	29km (18.0m)
Guidance	Command guidance in the 10cm band with AP-75 autopilot
Minimum effective range	8km (5m)
Maximum effective altitude	27km (16.7m)
Minimum effective altitude	500m (1,650ft)

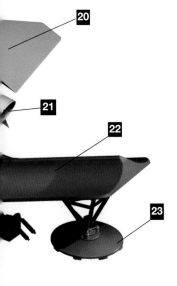

E: Camouflaged Dvina missiles

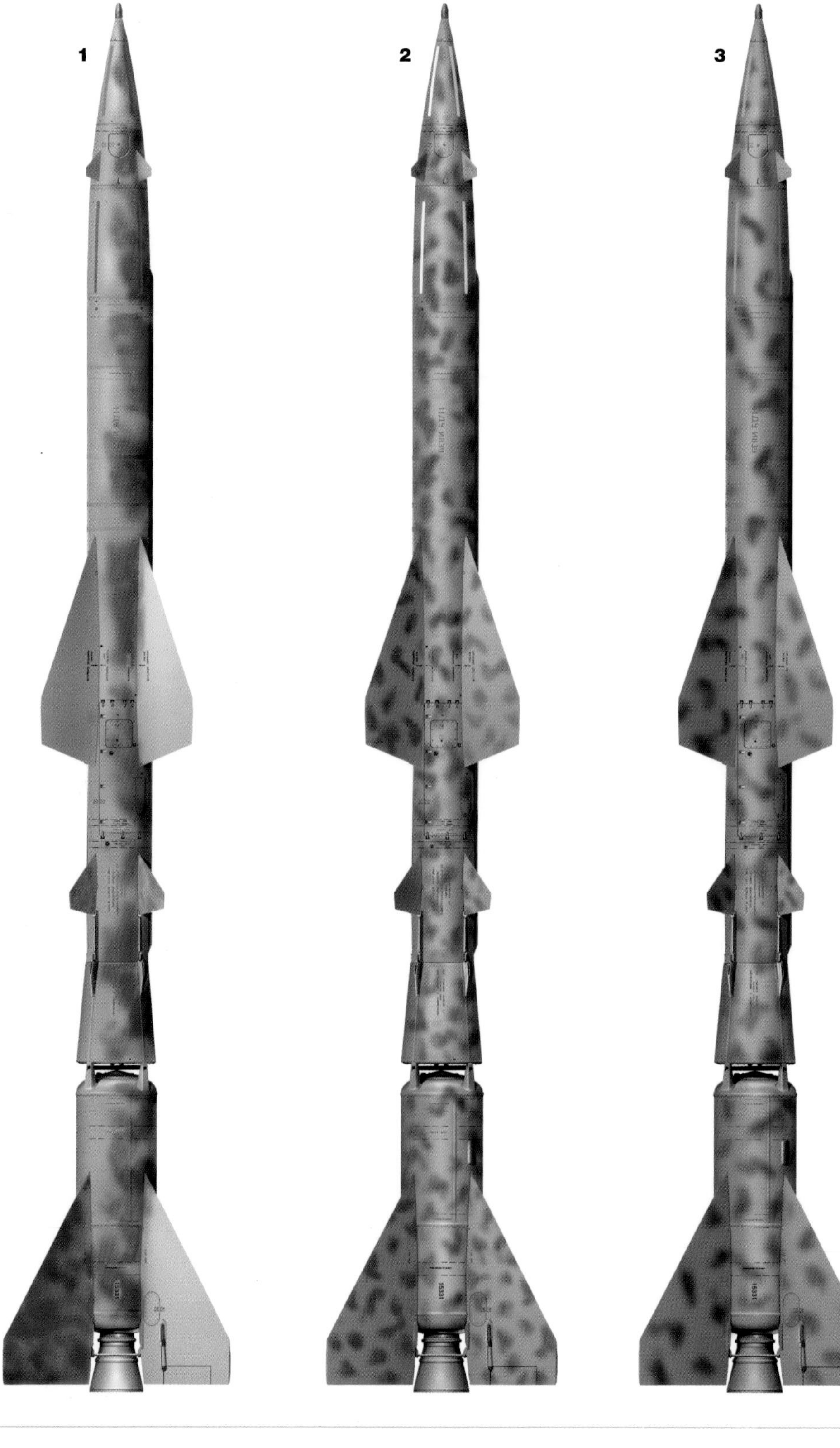

1

2

3

F: SA-2 launch battery, 236th SAM Regiment, North Vietnam, 1972

F

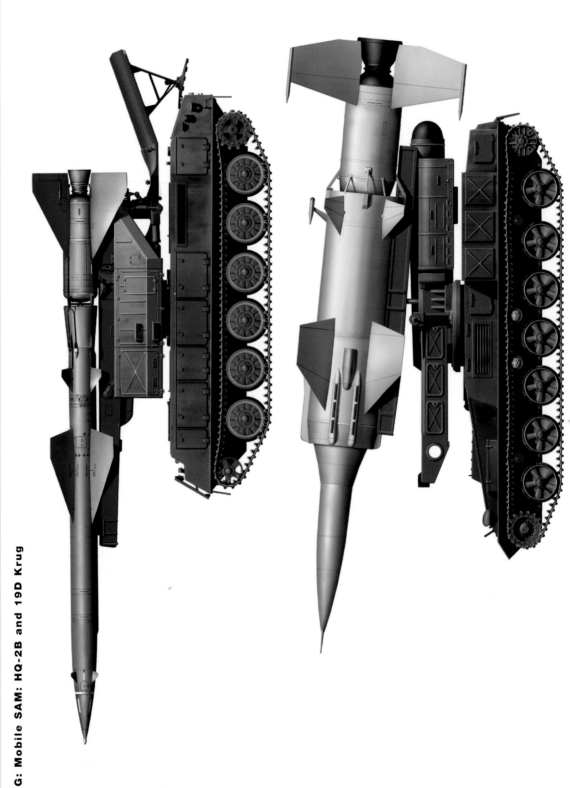

G: Mobile SAM: HQ-2B and 19D Krug

were launched in combat, and of the remaining 1,000, over 200 were lost on the ground-to-air strikes, about 600 were defective, and some were expended in training. The Soviet Union began providing two regiments of the newer S-125 in 1972, but neither regiment was trained or equipped in time to take part in the air campaign.

The Vietnam air war saw the largest use of SAMs in history and had a profound influence on the future of air combat. Even though the S-75 did not prove as effective as the Soviets had hoped, it significantly degraded the performance of US strike aircraft. Its design specifications called for a probability-of-kill of 80 percent with a three-round salvo, but actual combat performance was woefully short of that expectation. The SA-75MK Dvina version used in Vietnam was the oldest version of the S-75 system and the least resistant to electronic counter-measures. The mere presence of the SA-2 over Vietnam had a detrimental impact on US air operations, leading to what US air defense experts called "virtual attrition." Even if a SAM system did not shoot down many aircraft, its presence alone could accomplish the mission of defending a location by dissuading its opponents from attacking. The SA-2 sometimes was able to accomplish this in Vietnam, for example forcing SAC to abort about one-third of its B-52 missions over North Vietnam prior to *Linebacker II* because of the presence of SA-2 batteries. Besides its passive defensive value, the presence of SA-2 batteries further degraded tactical strike aviation by forcing the use of complicated electronic warfare tactics. Every bomb pylon taken up by a jammer pod was one less bomb carried to target. By the later stages of the war, it was not unusual for the electronic support aircraft in a strike package to actually outnumber the aircraft carrying bombs to the target area, all necessary to deal with

By the time of the 1973 war, many of the older Egyptian RSNA-75M radars had been upgraded to RSN-75V2 standards, including the "bird house" for optical tracking during intense electronic jamming. (US DoD)

the SA-2 threat, and wasting an enormous number of sorties. The passive attrition caused by the SAM batteries led USAF planners to think up new approaches to strike aviation. The most intriguing was Stealth, a strike aircraft using new technology that would make it invisible to SAM radars, so that it did not need either jammer pods or the accompaniment of electronic support aircraft. This eventually emerged in the late 1980s as the F-117 stealth strike fighter and the B-2 stealth bomber.

It is worth noting that both the US and USSR misunderstood some of the lessons of the air conflict. Soviet and North Vietnamese kill claims against US aircraft were wildly off the mark, about six times higher than actual shoot-downs, and so tended to overestimate the effectiveness of the SA-2. Likewise, the US tended to over-count the numbers of SAMs launched, about 9,000 estimated vs. 5,800 actually launched, thereby underestimating the performance of the SA-2.

OPERATION *KAVKAZ*: S-75 IN THE 1967–73 MIDDLE EAST WARS

In 1965, the Soviet Union agreed to sell the SA-75MK Dvina system to Egypt and by the time of the outbreak of the 1967 Six-Day War, a total of 27 batteries had arrived. With limited electronic warfare equipment, the Israeli air force countered the two Egyptian S-75 batteries in the Sinai by avoiding them or by exploiting their poor low-altitude coverage. About 12–20 missiles were fired, claiming nine aircraft kills, though only two Israeli aircraft were lost to SAMs. The Israelis captured about 12 launchers and other related equipment, much of it heavily damaged by air strikes.

The Egyptian air defense force was the first to use the S-75M Volkhov system in combat during the 1973 war, though it was outnumbered by the older Dvina and Desna versions. This 20D missile is seen on the SM-90 launcher. (US DoD)

The stereotypical deployment pattern of the S-75 system encouraged the Egyptian air defense force to protect the launchers and radar site with sand berms, like this site seen in the 1980s. (US DoD)

In the wake of the war, the Soviets agreed to build up the Egyptian force substantially. In July 1968, the Egyptians consolidated their Dvina units and other air defense equipment by forming an Air Defense Command, patterned after the Soviet PVO-Strany. By 1969, two brigades with seven batteries were stationed along the Suez Canal in the first phase of the War of Attrition with the Israeli Air Force. From July 1969 to March 1970, the Egyptian SAM units fired 36 missiles, claiming eight kills. Egyptian officers were not pleased with the shortcomings of the SA-75MK system, and in January 1970 the USSR agreed to a major modernization of Egyptian air defenses, including the improved S-75 Desna with 13D missile and the new S-125 Pechora. Codenamed Operation *Kavkaz* (*Caucasus*), Soviet PVO-Strany troops manned the new S-125 batteries to speed up the deployment of the new SAM belt. A new unit, the 18th Special SAM Division, was formed for this mission, better known as the "11th Dnepropetrovsk" since it was based on cadres from that division. The 18th Special consisted of three S-125 brigades, each with eight batteries with four launchers per battery. Many of the new S-125 batteries were deployed around key cities and military facilities in Egypt, but a few were forward deployed along the Suez Canal and so engaged with the Israeli Air Force.

By the summer of 1970, the Egyptian air defense forces had 13 S-75 and three S-125 batteries along the Canal, along with 20 new Strela-2 (NATO: SA-7) man-portable SAM platoons, a dozen new ZSU-23-4 Shilka air defense gun vehicles, and a substantial number of anti-aircraft guns. During the entire War of Attrition from 1969 to 1971, the Egyptian and Soviet SAM batteries took part in 124 engagements, using 264 missiles and claiming 32 aircraft kills; the Israeli Air Force acknowledged losing only 13 aircraft to both SAMs and guns during this period.

The Egyptian batteries sometimes camouflaged their missiles like this 11DMVK seen in the 1980s. (US DoD)

The War of Attrition set the stage for the October War of 1973, with Egypt using its reinforced SAM batteries as a shield against Israeli air power to permit the Egyptian army to cross the Suez Canal and retake the Sinai. Egypt shifted eight SAM brigades over the Canal with 54 S-75 and S-125 batteries from its total of 83 S-75 batteries and 45 S-125 batteries. Although the Egyptian SAM batteries were able to keep the Israeli Air Force at bay in the opening days of the Sinai campaign, an aggressive Israeli SEAD operation was able to burn holes through the Egyptian defenses to permit strikes against Egyptian army units by Israeli attack aircraft. In total, the Egyptians claimed 149 SAM kills, including 20 by the new Kvadrat (NATO: SA-6), seven to the man-portable Strela-2, 101 by S-75, and 21 by the S-125. The forward SAM batteries were the most vulnerable to counter-action, with the Israeli 175mm M107 self-propelled gun accounting for 13 of the 15 batteries lost on the east bank of the Suez. Israeli air attacks accounted for a further 18 batteries attacked on the west banks of the Suez. Israel estimated that it had destroyed 33 batteries by air attack and 11 by ground attack with a further 11 damaged, about one-third of the deployed Egyptian force.

At the same time, Syria struck the Golan Heights, its forces covered by some of its 19 SAM brigades: 11 strategic brigades (with four SA-75MK, 41 S-75M, and 42 S-125 batteries), and eight tactical brigades with 41 2K12 Kvadrat batteries and 47 Strela-2 platoons. Besides the 91 aircraft Syria claimed using the S-75 and S-125, they also claimed a further 64 aircraft, 46 using the 2K12 Kvadrat and 18 by the 9K32 Strela-2 tactical SAMs, for a grand total of 173 kills. Russian accounts suggest that Syrian SAM losses included three S-75 batteries, five S-125 batteries, and five 2K12 Kvadrat batteries. This is actually higher than the Israeli estimates of three destroyed by air attack, one by ground attack and five damaged by air attack.

The Egyptian and Syrian claims of 322 Israeli aircraft lost due to SAMs were excessive considering that total losses were only 102 aircraft, many of which were downed by anti-aircraft guns. Published analysis after the war suggested the total was closer to 40 Israeli losses to SAMs: two to S-75, four to S-125, six to Strela-2 and 28 to the new Kvadrat. The disproportionate impact of the Kvadrat and the poor performance of the S-75 and S-125 in these battles was strongly connected to Israeli use of ECM pods such as the US-supplied AN/ALQ-101-6 and ALQ-101-8. These ECM pods were designed to counteract the older Fan Song and Low Blow radars but not the Kvadrat's new 1S91 radar (Straight Flush), which worked on fundamentally different guidance principles. Curiously enough, as many as 15 of the Egyptian and Syrian aircraft losses were due to fratricide by their own S-75 and S-125 SAM batteries, and a further 44 to the deadly Kvadrat.

STRATEGIC SAMS IN THE 1967–73 MIDDLE EAST WARS

	Engagements	Missiles fired	Kills claimed
1967 war			
SA-75MK	10	15	9
1969–70 War of Attrition			
SA-75MK	108	231	23
S-125	16	35	9
1973 war: Egypt			
SA-75MK	140	400	90
S-75	29	88	8
S-75M	3	8	3
S-125	61	174	21
1973 war: Syria			
SA-75MK	50	116	26
S-75	60	139	32
S-125	72	131	33
Total	**549**	**1,337**	**254**

A rear view of an Egyptian RSN-75V radar in a concrete revetment. (US DoD)

FOREIGN GUIDELINES

In 1957, the Soviet government agreed to transfer license production rights for the SA-75 system to China, but this became entangled in China's deteriorating political relations with the USSR and the withdrawal of Soviet advisers in July 1960. In August 1961, the Bureau of Machinery and Electronics No.2 was set up in Shanghai to manage the program, now called the HQ-1 (Hong Qi-1: Red Flag). The first flight tests of HQ-1 missiles were conducted in June 1963, but problems with the RSNA-75 radar copy (NATO: Gin Sling) delayed service acceptance and limited production to only about four batteries per year in 1966–69. Chinese air defense batteries equipped with the Soviet-supplied SA-75s had been involved in a continuing series of engagements with RoCAF reconnaissance aircraft through much of the early 1960s, which made it clear that the SA-75 had serious limitations in terms of range and maximum altitude. As a result, in April 1965 a formal program began, intended to improve the HQ-1 as the HQ-2 to expand its operational envelope. The first HQ-2 missiles were delivered in July 1967, and on September 8, 1967, a RoCAF U-2 was shot down by one in east central China. When the HQ-2 was ready for mass production in the late 1960s, annual Chinese SAM production significantly increased from about four to about 25 batteries.

The HQ-2B was a mobile version of the HQ-2J, with the launcher mounted on a derivative of the Type 63 light tank chassis.

While work was underway on improvements to the HQ-2, the Great Cultural Revolution struck the Chinese aerospace industry, leading to purges of many of the design teams and factories and setting back most missile programs a decade or more. The HQ-2A missile entered development in 1973 to take advantage of lessons learned by Chinese advisers serving in Vietnam, who recognized that the missile needed to adapt to electronic warfare tactics. This program was substantially undermined through most of the early 1970s and not restarted until 1978. As a result, the HQ-2A was not accepted for production until 1984, by which time it was obsolete. Therefore, a second upgrade program began in 1978, the HQ-2B, which planned to move beyond the HQ-2A improvements and also aimed to reduce the excessive number of troops needed to operate an HQ-2 launch battery. The HQ-2B also introduced digital circuitry to replace older tube circuitry in the system, and introduced the improved

The 1960s generation of strategic SAMs including the S-75, S-125, and S-200 were finally replaced, starting in the 1980s, with the S-300P Volkhov (SA-10 Grumble) system. This shows a 5P85DU launcher of the S-300PMU-2 Favorit system.

ZD-2(B) radar. Two versions of the HQ-2B were fielded: the mobile HQ-2B which placed the launcher on a Type 63 light tank chassis, and the similar HQ-2J which used the standard semi-mobile launcher copied from the Soviet SM-63. These were the last major versions of the family produced in any significant numbers, and they were exported to a number of countries including Iran, Pakistan, and North Korea. Iran manufactured the HQ-2J under license as the Sayad-1 (SD-1) missile starting in the 1990s. China also developed a surface-to-surface version of the HQ-2B as an inexpensive alternative to the Soviet Scud missile, and this version was variously called Project 8610, B-610 or by its export name of M-7.

The US CIA replaced the U-2 with the supersonic SR-71 Blackbird reconnaissance aircraft in the mid-1960s. Although it was restricted from operations over the Soviet Union, the SR-71 was used in missions over China, Vietnam, and North Korea, where it was fired on more than 800 times by SA-2 missiles without a single hit. The Chinese Ministry of National defense authorized the development of a derivative of the HQ-2, the HQ-3, to deal with the Blackbird. This was supplied with a more powerful rocket sustainer and the substantially improved Song-9A radar. Flight tests were conducted in 1966–69, but like many programs it went into limbo due to the Cultural Revolution. It was followed by the substantially modified HQ-4 in the late 1970s, but in the end neither type was accepted for serial production.

FINAL REFINEMENTS

Even if the S-75 system had passed its prime by the late 1970s, there were still over 400 batteries deployed in the Soviet Union, providing an incentive for modest upgrades. One of the most obvious lessons of the air campaigns of the 1960s and 1970s was the need for an optical adjunct like that incorporated in the Vietnamese SA-75MK Dvina. An effort was undertaken in the mid-1970s to upgrade the more modern Volkhov versions with a 9Sh33A Karat-2 camera, along with modifications to the

As the Soviet PVO-Strany retired the S-75 for more modern systems, the equipment was transferred to client states, whether needed or not. This is an 11D missile on a PR-11A transporter-loader on parade in Kabul, Afghanistan in the 1970s. (US DoD)

The Iraqi air defense command used the S-75M Volkhov system during its war with Iran in 1980–88 but with little success due to the growing obsolescence of the system. Some were expended in a surface-to-surface role as the Al Fahd 300.

command guidance system to allow it to be used in a surface-to-surface mode like the US Army's Nike-Hercules SAM. The new version finished testing in November 1978 and it was accepted for service as the S-75M4 Volkhov. Many older Soviet systems were brought up to these standards.

There were a remarkably large number of sub-variants of the S-75 missiles built over the years. When originally introduced into service, the 11D missile had a nominal warranty of 18 months once loaded on its launcher. This was due to the fact that the corrosive oxidizer used in the propellant began to eat away at the seals, and the electronics of the time also suffered from environmental deterioration when the missile was left out in harsh weather. It soon became apparent that 18 months was too long and the warranty life was reduced to one year. At this point, the missile was sent back to factories for rebuilding. In some cases, the missile was simply refurbished, while in other cases it was refurbished and brought up to an improved standard. Taking the 20D (V-755) missile as an example, the new-production 20DS (V-755S) version introduced new guidance electronics that allowed the missile to engage targets as low as 656ft (200m). When some of the older 20D missiles were sent back for refurbishment, they also were upgraded with this feature, becoming the 20DA (V-755A). When the newer 20DS missiles were sent back for refurbishment, they were upgraded to the 20DSU standard, which had new electronics that made it faster to prepare the guidance for launch. Not all these myriad upgrades are covered in this book.

With the S-75 being slowly retired from Soviet service, some of the launch batteries were modernized and exported. The first of these export/upgrade programs was the S-75M Volga, which used the 20D missile of the Volkhov system and many but not all of the system upgrades. A total of 53 of these were sold to Syria in 1973–87 and 39 more for Libya in 1975–83.

The S-75 system was the most widely exported air defense missile system in history, with the exception of small man-portable missiles like the Strela-2 (SA-7 Grail). A total of over 600 batteries were exported to at least 30 countries, including over 20,000 missiles. The S-75 system took part in numerous wars after the 1973 Middle East conflict, but its effectiveness was declining. During the Iran-Iraq War of 1980–88, Iraq deployed the newer Volkhov-M2 version of the S-75 system, but Iranian sources state that it accounted for only five aircraft kills during the entire war. Cut off from Soviet supplies, Iran acquired SA-75 Dvina systems from Libya, but found them far less effective than the MIM-23 Hawk obtained from the US a decade earlier. Desperate for air defense systems, Iran finally acquired the Chinese HQ-2J in 1985, first using them in combat in early 1987. Their performance was so poor that Iranian crews joked that "if we fire enough of these giants, an Iraqi will fly into one sooner or later." Iraq continued to use its S-75 systems in later conflicts including the 1991 Gulf War, but with little success. During the wars in the Balkans in the 1990s, the Bosnian Serbs expended a number of missiles in an improvised surface-to-surface mode. One of the last known successes of the S-75 was in March 1993, when a Su-27 fighter was shot down during the conflict between Georgia and Abkahzia.

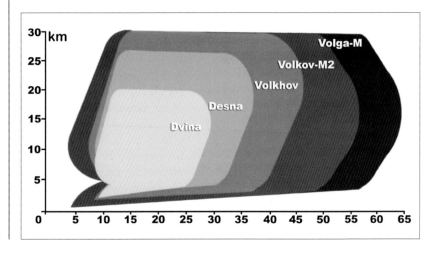

This chart shows the kill envelope of the various generations of the S-75 system. As can be seen, the trend was to extend the range and low-altitude performance of the system in successive generations.

S-75 VARIANTS AND DESIGNATIONS

System	Fakel	Industry	US+ NATO codename	Launcher	Standardization	Radar US	Radar Name
SA-75 Dvina	V-750	1D	SA-2a Guideline	SM-63	Dec 11, 1957	RSNA-75	Fan Song A
SA-75M Dvina	V-750V	11D	SA-2b Guideline Mod 1	SM-63-I	May 1958	RSNA-75M	Fan Song B
S-75N Desna	V-750VN	13D	SA-2c Guideline Mod 2	SM-63-I	May 22, 1959	RSN-75	Fan Song C
S-75D Desna	V-755	20D	(not designated)	SM-63-IIA	1969	RSN-75	Fan Song C
S-75M Volkhov	V-755	20D	SA-2d Guideline Mod 3	SM-90	April 20, 1961	RSN-75V	Fan Song E
S-75M Volkhov	V-760	15D	SA-2e Guideline Mod 4	SM-90	May 15, 1964	RSN-75V	Fan Song E
S-75M2 Volkhov	V-759	5Ya23	SA-2f Guideline Mod 5	SM-90	1968	RSN-75V2	Fan Song F
S-75M3 Volkhov	V-760V	5V29	(not designated)	SM-90	1975	RSN-75V3	(not designated)
S-75M4 Volkhov	V-759	5Ya23	(not designated)	SM-90	November 1978	RSN-75V4	(not designated)

SYSTEM PERFORMANCE

System	Missile	US designation	Max target speed (km/h)	Min altitude (km)	Max altitude (km)	Min range (km)	Max range (km)
SA-75 Dvina	1D	SA-2a	1,500	3	20	8	29
SA-75M Dvina	11D	SA-2b	1,500	3	22	8	29
S-75N Desna	13D	SA-2c	1,500	3	27	8	34
S-75M Volkhov	20D	SA-2d	2,300	1	30	7	43
S-75M2 Volkhov	5Ya23	SA-2f	3,600	0.3	30	6	56
S-75M4 Volkhov	5Ya23		3,600	0.2	30	6	56
S-75M Volga-M	5Ya23		3,600	0.1	30	6	67
HQ-2B		CSA-1	1,500	0.5	27	8	30

With so many export systems still active around the globe, in the mid-1990s Almaz offered an upgrade package for older S-75 systems, called the Volga-M, which replaced some of the old tube electronics with newer digital analogs. Few, if any, of these upgrades took place, as the system was widely recognized as obsolete and not worth the bother to upgrade. Nevertheless, the S-75 system was not formally retired from Russian service until 1999. The Russian PVO-Strany expended much of its remaining inventory as aerial targets as part of the RM-75 Lisa SAM training system and the Avangard plant converted old 20D missiles into the *Korshun* (Kite) and the 5Ya23 into the *Sinitsa* (Titmouse) missile targets.

FURTHER READING

The SA-2 Guideline has remained shrouded in mystery for most of its life. Recent Russian accounts have gone a long way to explaining its development, but some aspects of these programs, such as the modifications undertaken during the Vietnam war, still remain hidden. While there are no full-length books on the history of the SA-2, there has been a stream of excellent articles in Russian on its development and combat use. Since few readers of this book are likely to read Russian, I have translated the titles of the Russian articles listed below to more clearly convey their contents. The journal VKO is *Voenno-Kosmicheskaya Oborona* (Aerospace Defense) and ViZH is *Voenno-istoricheskiy Zhurnal* (Military History Journal).

There are numerous books on air campaigns of the past 50 years in which the SA-2 was involved, so this list is confined only to those that provide especially important coverage to the SA-2, for example, Michel's excellent book on *Linebacker*. For those readers perplexed about the intricacies of electronic warfare, Price's superb third volume on US electronic warfare is indispensable.

Articles

_____ "SA-75M against the B-52*," *VKO*, No.2 (15) (2004)

Chernov, Aleksandr, "Radar Units in Operation Linebacker-2*," *VKO*, No.5 (24) (2005)

Ganin, Sergey, Vladimir Korovin, *et al.*, "Sistema-75," *Tekhnika i vooruzhenie*, Nos 10, 12 (2002); No.1 (2003)

Gruszczynski, Jerzy, and Michal Fiszer, "Sistiema-75: Dwina, Desna, Wolchow," *Nowa Technika Wojskowa*, Nos 1, 2 (2004)

Korovin, Vladimir, "17D – The Flying Laboratory*," *Krylya Rodina*, No.1 (1994)

– "Towards Hypersonic Speeds*," *Krylya Rodina*, No.6 (1994)

Kostyunin, Aleksandr, "Aerial Battleships under Missile Fire*," *VKO*, No.2 (21) (2005)

Kyupenin, A. I., "Counterattack of the Vietnamese SAM Units against US Aviation in December 1972*," *ViZh*, No.8 (2005)

– "Organization of USAF Electronic Countermeasures during Operation *Linebacker-2*," *ViZh*, No.7 (2005)

Malgin, Aleksandr, and M. Malgin, "Maneuver as a Means of Survival: Lessons of Mobile SAM Defense in Vietnam 1964–1973*," *VKO*, No.4 (23) (2005)

– "Formation of Vietnam's Air Defense Force*," *VKO*, No.3 (28) (2006)

Mikhaylov, Andrey, "Combat Unit Operations: From Engineering Support and Camouflage to Missile Re-supply in Combat*," *VKO*, No.3 (28) (2006)

– "The Battles after the War of Attrition*," *VKO*, No.5 (24) (2005)

– "The Eleven-Day Campaign*," *VKO*, No.6 (19) (2004)

– "Statistics on SAM Combat Launches*," *VKO*, No.6 (25) (2005)

Pribbenow, Merle, "The –Ology War: Technology and Ideology in the Vietnamese Defense of Hanoi," *Journal of Military History*, No.67 (January 2003)

Sergiyevskiy, Anatoliy, "An Unpopular Blackbird*," *VKO*, No.3 (16) (2004)

– "Prairie Fire*," *VKO*, No.4 (17) (2004)

Sokolov, Anatoliy, "Ambushes by Missile Crew*," *VKO*, No.6 (13) (2003)

– "Arab-Israeli Wars*," *VKO*, No.2 (5) (2002)

– "PVO in Local Wars and Armed Conflicts: Vietnam*," *VKO*, No.1 (1) (2001)

– "PVO in Local Wars and Armed Conflicts: The Arab-Israeli Wars*," *VKO*, No.2 (2) (2001)

Tkachev, Viktor, "Battles over the Suez Canal*," *VKO*, No.3 (16) (2004)

Zaloga, Steven, "Defending the Capitals: The First Generation of Soviet Strategic Air Defense Systems 1950–60," *Journal of Slavic Military Studies*, Vol. 10, No.4 (December 1997)

Books

Ganin, Sergey, Vladimir Korovin, *et al.*, *Missile Systems of the PVO-Strany**, Aviatsiya i Kosmonavtika (2002)

Kolesnik, N. N. *et al.*, *War Over Vietnam: How It Was in the Memories of Soviet Veterans 1965–1973**, Ekzamen (2005)

Michel, Marshall L. III, *America's Last Vietnam Battle: The 11 Days of Christmas*, Encounter (2002)

Pedlow, Gregory and Donald Welzenbach, *The CIA and the U-2 Program 1954–1974*, CIA (1998)

Pervov, Mikhail, *SAMs for National Air Defense**, AviaRus-21 (2001)

Price, Alfred, *The History of US Electronic Warfare, Vol. III: Rolling Thunder Through Allied Force 1964–2000*, Association of Old Crows (2000)

Svetlov, Vladimir and Vladimir Korovin, *Fakel's Missiles*, Fakel (2003)

Zaloga, Steven, *Soviet Air Defense Missiles: Design, Development, and Tactics*, Jane's (1989)

Zolotarev, V. A. (ed.), *Russia (USSR) in Local Conflicts in the Second Half of the 20th Century**, Military History Institute of the Russian Ministry of Defense (2000)

*Russian titles translated into English.

An Egyptian Dvina battery reloads its SM-63 launcher from a PR-11B transporter-loader semi-trailer, towed by a ZIL-157KV truck. (US DoD)

COLOR PLATE COMMENTARY

A: THE SA-2 MISSILE

This plate shows the basic versions of the SA-2 missile, the 11D (1), 20D (2), and 5Ya23 (3). The missiles were initially painted in an overall aluminum color, though by the early 1960s when the 20D entered production, some plants had begun to shift to a pale gray instead. Also at this time, some plants began to paint the center instrument compartment and solid fuel booster in gloss white to improve reflectivity against the sun. The final production runs of the 5Ya23 were generally finished in overall light gray paint.

B: DVINA LAUNCHER

This plate shows the basic Dvina (SA-2b) firing unit, consisting of an 11D missile mounted on the SM-63-I launcher. The missile is in the initial overall aluminum paint finish, while the launcher is finished in the standard Soviet dark olive green. The launcher seldom had any external markings, though there was stenciling inside the compartments.

C: OPERATION *GRAND SLAM*: U-2 OVER SVERDLOVSK, MAY 1, 1960

This plate shows the interception of Gary Powers' U-2 over Sverdlovsk by a Desna battery of the 4th Independent PVO-Strany Army. The 13D missile of the Desna system was essentially identical to the more familiar 11D, differing in the electronics since it operated on a different frequency band. The solid fuel booster dropped off about four seconds after launch, at which point the liquid-fuel sustainer engine ignited as seen here.

D: DVINA SYSTEM

The Dvina system used a single-rail launcher, the SM-63-I, developed by one of Leningrad's premier artillery design bureaus, Central Design Bureau-34 (TsKB-34) headed by

RSN-75/Fan Song Variants

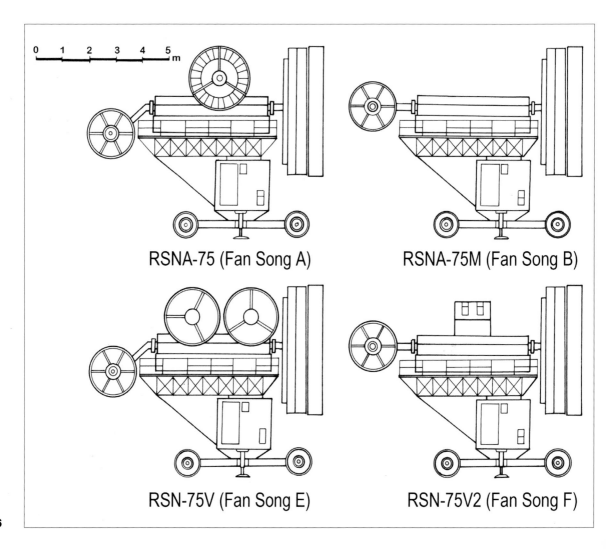

RSNA-75 (Fan Song A)

RSNA-75M (Fan Song B)

RSN-75V (Fan Song E)

RSN-75V2 (Fan Song F)

I. I. Ivanov. Traverse of the launcher and elevation of the launch rail was provided by electric motors housed in the two containers on either side of the launch rail. The 11D missile as seen here was a two-stage design, with an initial solid fuel motor providing the impulse off the launcher, followed by a liquid rocket sustainer as its principal power-plant. It is worth noting that both the 11D missile of the Dvina system and the 13D missile of the Desna system were externally almost identical and shared the same launcher, except for minor differences in electronics connected with the guidance system.

E: CAMOUFLAGED DVINA MISSILES

The Soviet PVO-Strany recommended against camouflage painting the missiles since it led to unwanted heat build-up inside of them if left deployed in the sun. Nonetheless, some armies did camouflage their missiles, since the reflective aluminum paint finish tended to make them too visible from the air. The 11DU missile (1) served in the Egyptian Air Defense Command in the 1973 war and the finish consists of a very irregular pattern of sand, dark green, and brown, with the underbelly and some of the fins left in the original light gray finish. The 11DMVK (2) is another Egyptian example from the 1980s, showing an overall gray-green finish with dark brown splotches. The 11DMV missile (3) is a Czechoslovakian example from the 1990s in an overall olive green finish with brown splotches.

F: SA-2 LAUNCH BATTERY, 236TH SAM REGIMENT, NORTH VIETNAM, 1972

Since the North Vietnamese Dvina batteries moved so often, they were seldom protected by earthen berms as was the recommended practice. The North Vietnamese tended to camouflage paint their 11D missiles to reduce their visibility to aerial reconnaissance, usually in a pattern of dark green blotches over a medium olive green; in this case foliage has been added as well.

G: MOBILE SAM: HQ-2B AND 19D KRUG

China offered a mobile version of its HQ-2 system, the HQ-2B, with the missile and launcher mounted on a modified Type 63 light tank chassis (top). Although this could be used in the SAM role, it was intended as an expedient surface-to-surface missile for customers such as Iran, which was cut off from the supply of Soviet Scud missiles during the bitter 1980–88 war with Iraq. These missiles were sometimes finished in colors other than the usual light gray, in this case, a medium blue-gray.

The vehicle on the bottom is the final evolution of the SA-2 family, the 19D missile. This was a further development of the ram-jet-powered 17D family, offered for the Soviet Ground Forces Krug (SA-4 Ganef) missile requirement and mounted on a modified Obiekt 123 tracked launcher. Ultimately, the rival KS-40 (3M8) missile developed by V. P. Yefremov's NII-20 was selected for production, but the 19D was test-fired several times in 1961–62.

One of the lingering mysteries of the Vietnamese employment of the S-75 system was the persistent report by US pilots of a "Fat Albert" version of the missile seen several times in combat in the later years of the war. There have been suggestions that it might have been an experimental deployment of the Krug (SA-4) or even a combat trial of experimental S-75 missiles such as the ram-jet powered Fakel 17D missile. The "Fat Albert" missiles remain a mystery.

The S-75 launcher could be moved by attaching wheeled suspension modules to the cruciform base. This Polish SM-63-II is shown protected with the usual canvas tarp.

INDEX